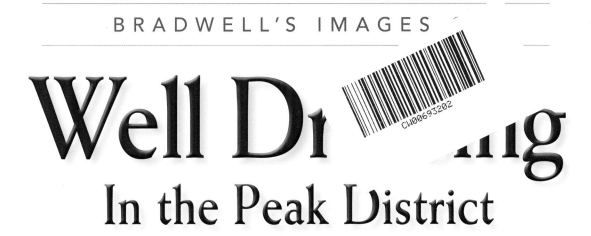

Well Dressing
In the Peak District

Text by Louise Maskill

Images by Mark Titterton

BRADWELL
BOOKS

Published by Bradwell Books

9 Orgreave Close Sheffield S13 9NP

books@bradwellbooks.co.uk

1st Edition

ISBN: 9781912060658

Design by: Mark Titterton

Text by: Louise Maskill

Photography: Mark Titterton

Print: Gomer Press, Llandysul, Ceredigion SA44 4JL

Front Cover: Hands Well, Tissington

Back Cover: Uniting Church Well Dressing, Whaley Bridge

Page 1: Smalldale Well Dressing, Bradwell

Contents

Introduction

The well dressings of the English Peak District attract thousands of visitors to the villages of Derbyshire and Staffordshire throughout the summer. From May to September many villages in the National Park and the surrounding area decorate their wells, springs, fountains, standpipes, taps and other public water sources, with communities coming together to design, create and display these ephemeral works of art.

Buxworth Well Dressing

The Peak District National Park was the first national park in the United Kingdom, created in 1951 to conserve and enhance the unique geology, natural beauty, wildlife and cultural heritage of the area. The National Park covers 555 square miles and includes parts of the counties of Derbyshire, Yorkshire, Staffordshire and Cheshire, with the custom of well dressing extending across much of the region.

The origins of this ancient ritual are obscure, with theories ranging from pagan veneration of water deities to medieval celebrations after a community's survival of the Black Death or other scourge. The custom had almost died

Petaling the Well Dressing - Tissington

out by the late eighteenth century, but it was readopted in a few places and has undergone a recent revival to form part of the annual round of community celebration in settlements across Derbyshire and Staffordshire.

Well dressings are now a fixture on the yearly calendar in over one hundred places, often coinciding with the location's Wakes Week celebration. The name refers to the wake which was part of the religious observance of local patron saints' days, with many places traditionally staging all-night vigils (or wakes) for prayer and reflection; these were sometimes extended to include public entertainments or games.

The extension of this one- or two-day event into the week-long community celebration of Wakes Week dates from the Industrial Revolution in the north of England and the Midlands, when local factories, collieries and mills closed for a week, often for maintenance. The workers in the nearby villages and towns made this enforced and often unpaid layoff into an opportunity, turning it into a regular summer holiday event with bands, games, funfairs, daytrips (often to the seaside at places like Blackpool or Skegness) – and in the Peak District, of course, the dressing of the local wells.

Many hours of work and communal effort go into the design and production of the dressings themselves, and when they are complete they are displayed around the town or village at the current or historical sites of public water sources such as wells, taps or springs. They attract visitors from near and far and often raise awareness of local issues, as well as bringing in money for charities or good causes in the area. They last around a week before the clay and natural items used in their construction start to crumble and decay, at which point they are dismantled and the frames are cleaned and stored ready for use in future years.

This book will introduce you to this fascinating and enduring custom and the traditions associated with it, as well as showcasing some of the intricate designs from previous years and the beautiful towns and villages where they are created.

Detail from the Spring Gardens Well Dressing, Buxton

The History
of Well Dressing

The archaic custom of well dressing may once have been practised much more widely than its modern-day focus in the Peak District counties of Derbyshire and Staffordshire. It is generally assumed that it has pagan or Roman origins, with sacrifices or votive offerings to water deities gradually evolving into veneration by decoration of water sources. There is an associated tradition in other areas which sees rags, ribbons or scraps of cloth (known as clooties) tied on and around wells and water sources, but nowhere else is the survival of the ritual as elaborate, seasonal or communal as in the Peak District.

As with many other pre-Christian rituals the early church absorbed and adapted this practice of water worship, although this may have been a slow and controversial process; as late as 960 a decree forbade the veneration of fountains, and St Anselm condemned the practice as idolatry in 1102.

Rowsley Well Dressing

The survival of the custom in the Peak District but almost nowhere else in the country may be explained in part by the porous geology of the local rocks. Precious water from rainfall soaks through the limestone bedrock very quickly, leaving soils and water courses dry. Celebration and thanksgiving for reliable water sources would have been particularly important where there was the ever-present threat of drought, and so the custom survived in isolated communities in the limestone Peak District long after it had disappeared from the rest of the UK.

Another aspect which may have contributed to the longevity of the ritual has to do with the long-known curative qualities of the local water, particularly in towns such as Buxton, Matlock, Ashbourne and Bakewell. Eighteenth-century health tourists, often travelling long distances to take the waters for ills such as tuberculosis or rheumatism, subscribed to a centuries-old belief in the health-giving qualities of the local wells or springs – for which the locals had long given thanks. Indeed, one of the few well dressings outside the Peak District takes place in Malvern, which has a tradition of water cures dating back to the twelfth century.

The practice experienced a patchy revival in the eighteenth and nineteenth centuries, with towns such as Buxton decorating new or renovated public sources of clean water provided by local benefactors. However, the current renewal of enthusiasm began in the twentieth century during the folklore revival. There have been breaks in continuity – for example, most communities did not decorate their wells during the two world wars in the last century – but this traditional country custom is alive and thriving in the twenty-first century. In certain locations there are local families who are born to it and who keep the community commitment strong, such as the Shimwell family in Stoney Middleton and Tideswell, and at the time of writing there is a total of over one hundred venues listed on the welldressing. com website.

The religious focus continues today, with most well dressings being blessed by the local church in a special community ceremony. Many displays have a religious theme in their design, although more secular subjects are becoming more common. These non-religious themes reflect local, national and sometimes international concerns, with examples of local anniversaries, social, environmental and even political issues being represented in recent years.

The well dressing year begins in May with early celebrations at places such as Tissington and Endon and continues through the summer, concluding with the final few decorations being produced in September at places such as Wormhill and Foolow. The dressings are mostly decorated with natural materials such as bark, moss, flower petals, leaves, seeds and crushed minerals impressed into a clay background, and sources of particular hard-to-find colours are highly prized, often kept secret and sometimes disputed between neighbouring communities. The decorations are intended to last at least a week, and are watered regularly to keep the clay moist. However, the boards are often left in place long after the colours have faded, the clay has dried and cracked and the designs have blown away – impermanent reminders of an enduring tradition.

Bath House Gardens Well Dressing, Stoney Middleton

Over Haddon Well Dressing

Soaking the boards, Tissington village pond

Puddling clay, Tissington

The Making of the Wells

The production of a well dressing begins with the decision on the year's theme. Sometimes a town or village will decide on an overarching theme; other places leave this up to the individual teams of volunteer well dressers. However the decision is made, for each well dressing a design is chosen and drawn out at full size on tracing paper.

Applying the clay, Tissington

Meanwhile, the preparation of the boards gets under way. Well dressings are usually composed of multiple panels, constructed of strong boards with raised frames around the edges. These must be thoroughly soaked so they are completely waterlogged; this is often done in a village pond (as at Tissington) or in a river (as at Youlgrave, presumably with the boards carefully tethered to stop them floating away, raft-like).

The soaking means that the boards are better able to support and keep moist the layer of clay which is applied next. The clay, locally sourced if possible and sometimes recycled from previous years, is puddled with water and salt to a smooth plastic consistency. (Local children often find this to be the best part of the process, since it involves bare feet, lots of trampling and getting muddy to the knees.)

The boards are studded with nails standing about half an inch proud of the wooden surface, to give the clay layer a firm key. The boards are laid flat and the puddled clay is applied to them; sometimes it is literally flung, to drive out air and ensure good adherence. (Children both young and old may also enjoy this bit.)

Pricking through the design, Eyam

Once applied, the clay is smoothed into a layer around an inch thick and is allowed to set slightly before the next phase, when the design is laid over the clay and the lines pricked through with a suitable implement (an awl or pinwheel). Then the paper is removed and the process of marking out begins; liners, traditionally black alder cones (known in Derbyshire as blacknobs), maize or beans, are pressed into the perforations in the clay to create the outline of the design.

Outlining the design, Eyam

Petaling, Eyam

Then the decoration proper commences. Natural materials, locally gathered and reflecting the colours in the design, are applied to the clay, with many hands making light work – well dressers tend to work in teams of around twelve, with children from local schools often involved as well. A critical requirement at this stage is that such things as petals or leaves must overlap and allow rain to run off the image, like roof tiles; for this reason, colours are applied by working from the bottom of the design to the top. Lichens and moss create shading, sheep's wool may be used for hair or beards, and crushed eggshell for skin tone.

Hours of painstaking work over four or five days will see the designs complete and ready for transport to their final locations. This is done with extreme care, often utilising a tractor and trailer. Assembling the dressing is a feat of engineering, with the extremely heavy boards needing to be winched or lifted into a vertical position, bolted together, and then held safely and securely in place to avoid collapse.

The completed dressings will remain in place for up to a week, tended by volunteers to answer visitors' questions, look after the charity collection boxes and mist the designs with water to put off the inevitable decay and drying-out for as long as possible. At the end of the display the dried-out clay is scraped out and collected, and the boards are taken down and transported to a barn or outhouse where they will be stored until the following year.

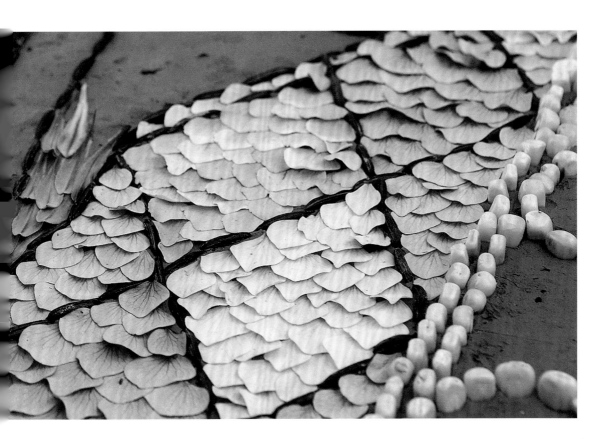

Petaling, Eyam

Assembling Town End Well Dressing, Eyam

Blessing the Wells

The blessing of well dressings is an integral part of the ritual. Most towns and villages stage a procession around the sites of the wells, led by the clergy and often with local bands or church choirs in attendance. In places where the well dressing celebrations involve a carnival, the weekend's royalty also take part in the procession as one of their duties. The church service, procession and blessings bring the community together to celebrate their effort, communal spirit, and the history and natural beauty of their local environs.

JESUS
FEEDS THE FIVE THOUSAND
THIS LITTLE BOY IS OFFERING HIS FOOD TO JESUS
1952-
2017
2 FISHES
WELL
Town Well

Blessing the Town Well, Tissington

Tissington Well Blessing

In Ashford in the Water a blessing ceremony is held on Trinity Sunday, the first Sunday after Pentecost or Whitsunday (the fiftieth day after Easter), which usually falls in late May or early June. A sermon is preached in the churchyard from the steps of the old preaching cross (weather permitting!). Then each of the village's six wells is visited and blessed in a procession led by the Bakewell Silver Band, the town clergy and the choir.

Tissington's well dressing activities centre around Ascension Day, usually in early to mid-May, with the village justly proud of the antiquity of its tradition (perhaps the oldest in Derbyshire). Local lore suggests that the village began well dressing, possibly as a revival of a half-remembered pagan custom, in thanksgiving for its deliverance from the Black Death in 1348-9, which was attributed to the village's pure water supply. Alternatively, some believe that Tissington well dressing began around 1615, when a severe drought ravaged the land but Tissington was saved by its reliable water sources. Whichever is true (and it is likely that we will never know), the village blesses its five wells in a special service and ceremony on Ascension Day, the fortieth day after Easter.

In Wirksworth the whole town celebrates with a carnival weekend over the late Spring Bank Holiday (originally the dressings were focused on Whitsuntide, the week after Whitsunday). The carnival runs in support of the well dressings; early in the week the wells are blessed in a service conducted over each one, attended by the carnival royalty and the town mayor as well as the local clergy, and over the Bank Holiday weekend the whole town turns out for a fair, a carnival parade through the town, live music and activities for all the family.

The village of Eyam is known for the inhabitants' heroism during the plague outbreak of 1665-66. Led by the rector, William Mompesson, the villagers quarantined themselves from the local community to prevent the spread of the plague which had reached the village via rats and fleas in a shipment of cloth from London. About a third of the village population, over 260 people, died in the outbreak, but their tragic sacrifice was effective; the plague spread no further in Derbyshire, certainly saving countless lives.

The three wells in Eyam are blessed as part of the village's carnival, with themes often reflecting the villagers' enduring sorrow and pride in their forbears' heroism. The carnival falls over the last weekend in August; a procession departs from the church on the Sunday, known as Plague Sunday, and visits the village's three wells, accompanied by the carnival royalty. The day's festivities conclude with an open-air ceremony at the natural amphitheatre of Cucklett Delph, where William Mompesson preached during the village's quarantine to avoid gatherings in the close confines of the church.

Finally in this whistle-stop tour of Peak District well blessings, perhaps one of the most eccentric is the Flash teapot service and parade. Flash is an isolated settlement which holds the title of the highest village in England, and the Flash Teapot Club was formed two centuries ago as a way to support local families in need. Villagers all contributed to a fund which was kept in a teapot, and emptied for use when any of them fell into hardship. The Teapot Parade commemorates this local social security effort, and visits the village's single well dressing on its way to the pub.

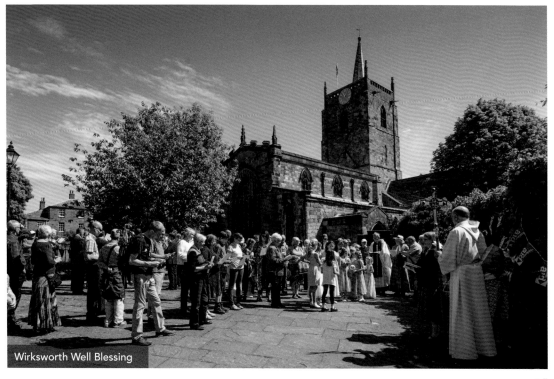

Wirksworth Well Blessing

Well Dressings Around the Peak District

Buxton

The town of Buxton is just outside the boundary of the National Park, but it is one of the most important towns in the western and central Peak. It has been an important site of pilgrimage and spa tourism since Roman times, but the first great boom in its fortunes began in the eighteenth century with the construction of the magnificent Crescent by the Fifth Duke of Devonshire, and took off properly in 1863 with the arrival of the railways.

The public water sources at Buxton have been dressed since 1840, when fresh water was made available at the Market Place drinking fountain as part of the Sixth Duke of Devonshire's continuing project of gentrification. Local people arranged a floral decoration, a tea party and a brass band procession, and the tradition of well dressing in Buxton was born.

In more recent times the town begins its celebrations in early July with a community service to bless its three wells, followed by a carnival weekend incorporating a road race organised by the local running club, a parade led by the Well Dressing Queen and her retinue, marching bands, a fun fair and entertainment for the whole family.

1917   2017

ST. MARY'S
CHURCH

Main Well Dressing, Little Longstone

Longstone and Hope

Village Well Dressing, Great Longstone

The neighbouring villages of Great and Little Longstone, near the Monsal Trail and the famous viewpoint at Monsal Head, decorate one well each – on the village green in Great Longstone, and at the village pump near the Packhorse pub in Little Longstone. Both communities celebrate in mid-July with music, a blessing service, church fêtes and refreshments.

Meanwhile, the village of Hope, at the centre of the beautiful Hope Valley in the northern Peak, dresses its four wells during its Wakes Week in late June. The Wakes Royalty are crowned, the wells are blessed and the village stages a week of concerts, sporting events, community workshops and scarecrow displays, culminating in carnival day with a procession and fireworks in the evening.

Edale Road Well Dressing, Hope

St Peter's Church Well Dressing, Hope

This page: Eyam **Opposite page:** Cressbrook

Eyam and Cressbrook

The 'plague village' of Eyam decorates three wells quite late in the season, usually at the end of August or the beginning of September. The wells are blessed in a ceremony at the start of Eyam's Wakes Week, which ends with the village carnival weekend and the open-air service of commemoration and thanksgiving for the many lives lost during the plague outbreaks of 1665/6, and the villagers' heroic sacrifice in quarantining themselves to preserve surrounding settlements.

The former mill village of Cressbrook, in the beautiful and historic Monsal Dale, grew up during the Industrial Revolution around a textile mill built alongside the River Wye by Richard Arkwright and later owned by William Needham, the so-called Minstrel of the Peak. Along with Litton Mill around a mile away, these industrial complexes were the sites of scandalous and harsh treatment of workhouse children brought as indentured labour from London.

Cressbrook and Litton dress two wells each, both in mid-June, celebrating with a week of gala events and Cressbrook and Wakes Week in Litton, incorporating music, maypole dancing, bands, refreshments, stalls and a torchlit procession through Cressbrook village on the final gala night.

Youlgrave

The village of Youlgrave (sometimes Youlgreave) stands on the hillside above the confluence of Lathkill and Bradford Dales, close to the Limestone Way, a 46-mile long-distance walking route which heads south from Castleton to end in the Dove Valley near Rocester. As such it is a popular stopping off point for hikers and walkers.

Youlgrave stages one of the larger well dressing events, decorating six wells or public taps to commemorate the piping of fresh water to the Fountain in the centre of the village in 1829, freeing villagers from the need to toil up the hill from the river to bring water. The village water is provided by Youlgreave Water Works Limited, one of the country's few private water supply companies, and is reputed never to have failed – a reason for celebration indeed!

The dressings are displayed around 24 June, the Feast of St John the Baptist, and are some of the largest in Derbyshire. Unlike in some locations, visitors to Youlgrave are welcome to help in the making of the well dressings in the week before the decorations are erected at their display sites – a great opportunity to experience and be part of this unique custom for yourself!

Wirksworth

The ancient leadmining and quarrying town of Wirksworth, at the southern end of the limestone plateau, is one of the oldest settlements in the Peak District. The area was an important industrial site at least as far back as the Romans, the town's Market Charter was granted by Edward I in 1306, and the town still holds an annual miners' court known as the Bar Moot (now Barmote) to govern all matters related to lead mining.

Wirksworth has dressed its water sources since 1827 when water was first piped to the town. The well dressing weekend over the Spring Bank Holiday in late May coincides with the town's Carnival, with processions, stalls, music, sports and many other activities.

The wells are blessed in a service starting at St Mary's Church in the centre of the town, the Carnival Royalty are crowned, and the entire town comes out to celebrate. Wirksworth usually decorates around ten wells, making this one of the largest celebrations in the Peak District – well worth a visit and a look around this historic town.

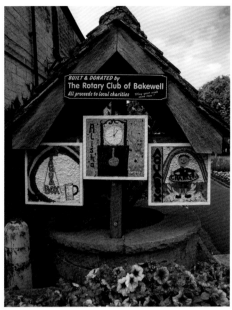

Bakewell

The small market town of Bakewell, on the River Wye in the heart of the Peak District, is famous for the invention of the Bakewell Pudding (not tart!), attributed to the cook at the Rutland Arms Hotel in the town around 1820 (although the exact details are disputed). The Old Original Bakewell Pudding Shop in the town still sells the dessert, baked on the premises to the original (closely guarded) recipe.

However, there is much more to Bakewell than puddings. The town has a rich industrial history, as well as being a spa town famous for its health-giving waters. Well dressing in Bakewell was revived in 1971, and is now a firm fixture in the community calendar as part of the town's carnival week in June or July each year. Bakewell decorates six wells, with a blessing ceremony that starts in the Garden of Remembrance. The carnival week includes processions, marching bands, a raft race, fancy dress, community sports and games (dominoes are popular!) and fun for all the family – something for everyone!

Ashford in the Water and Hayfield

Ashford in the Water stands on the River Wye and is widely regarded as one the prettiest villages in Derbyshire. It is known for the quarrying of Ashford Black marble and the picturesque Sheepwash Bridge, but also for the curious custom of maiden's garlands. These wreaths of paper flowers, rosettes and ribbons were made as funeral mementos following the deaths of female virgins and carried in front of their coffins in funeral processions. Some examples are displayed in the village church. Ashford dresses its six village wells around Trinity Sunday in early to mid-June, celebrating with a community service, music, and a flower festival in Holy Trinity Church in the village.

The village of Hayfield in the High Peak, known as the Gateway to Kinder and the Peaks from Stockport and Manchester, decorates six wells in late June or early July. The village has a history of textile and clothing manufacture, and it is a popular walking and mountain biking centre, lying on the Pennine Bridleway and providing access to the Kinder Scout plateau and the spectacular Kinder Downfall waterfall.

This page: Ashford in the Water **Opposite page:** Hayfield

28

Tideswell and Tissington

Tideswell well dressings form an integral part of the Tideswell Wakes Week (known locally and fondly as the Tidza Wakes), a nine-day festival which starts on the Saturday closest to the saints' day of St John the Baptist on 24 June. In Tideswell the Wakes are said to have been celebrated for 750 years, with well dressings revived as part of the festivities in the 1940s. The entire village participates in the Wakes celebrations, culminating on 'Big Saturday' with a procession, stalls, food, displays, and a marching band playing the unique Tideswell Processional. There is even a Battle of Britain flyover!

Finally, no tour of the Peak District's well dressing celebrations would be complete without a visit to Tissington, the village which claims to be the home of well dressing. Local lore states that the tradition has been practised here almost annually since 1348, when the village escaped the ravages of the Black Death and ascribed its deliverance to the purity of the local water supply. The village is one of the earliest to dress its water sources, in May each year, and provides a splendid start to the year's celebrations across the Peak District.

This page: Tideswell **Opposite page:** Tissington

RHS Chatsworth and Hartington

2017 saw the first RHS Well Dressing Competition, staged as part of the inaugural RHS Chatsworth Flower Show in June. The overarching theme for the flower show was Design Revolutionaries, and five designs on this theme with a local focus were selected for construction, display and public voting by visitors to the show.

The entry that won the public vote came from the town of Bakewell, depicting the nineteenth century Gothic revival magnificence of Burton Closes Hall. Other entries celebrated designers such as Brunel, Stephenson and Paxton, iconic local attractions like the Buxton Pavilion Gardens and the Great Conservatory at Chatsworth, and industrial and community links across Derbyshire. It is to be hoped that this is an event which will be repeated in years to come.

Other wells also celebrate wider themes; the village of Hartington decorates two wells, one of which in 2017 paid tribute to the role of bees in helping to pollinate and perpetuate the flowers and natural products which go into the production of the wells themselves. The message from Hartington in 2017? Save the bee!

Left: RHS Chatsworth **Above:** Hartington